About this book

If you had been a Roman child two thousand years ago, you would have worn a toga, eaten party food such as dormice stuffed with pine nuts, and watched bloodthirsty gladiator fights at the Colosseum during the holidays. But some things were just like life today. You would probably have played marbles, lived in a centrally-heated house, and gone to school.

In 753 BC, the story goes, Rome was founded by Romulus. He and his brother Remus had a very exciting start in life. They were brought up by a she-wolf! You can see a statue of them with the wolf on the next page. But however Rome really started, it grew from a village of huts into a great city. By the time Jesus Christ was born, the powerful Roman armies had conquered most of the known world. Then in 410 AD barbarians invaded Rome and the empire collapsed.

The pictures and descriptions in this book show you what it was like to grow up in Rome itself during its days of greatness.

Some of the words printed in *italics* may be new to you. You can look them up in the word list on page 92.

Growing up in Ancient Rome

AMANDA PURVES

Wayland

Growing up in Other Times

Frontispiece:
Romulus and Remus, the founders
of Rome, nursed by a wolf.

ISBN 0 85340 542 5
Copyright © 1978 by Wayland (Publishers) Ltd
First published in 1978 by Wayland (Publishers) Ltd,
49 Lansdowne Place, Hove, East Sussex, England. BN3 1HF
Text set in 12 pt. VIP Univers by Trident Graphics Ltd, Reigate, Surrey
Printed in Great Britain by Gale and Polden Ltd, Aldershot, and bound by
The Pitman Press Ltd, Bath

Contents

1. The Roman Family

The Ancient Romans had many more children than we do today. But many babies died when they were only a few days or weeks old because there were no proper drugs or hospitals to cure serious illnesses. Few people lived past the age of forty. So Romans crammed a lot into their short lives. Boys were considered grown up by the time they were fourteen, and girls when they were only twelve!

Slaves were very important to every family. Rich people had hundreds, but even the poor could afford a few. Children were brought up by nurses or slaves. Grandparents and unmarried relatives lived with the family, too. It was very crowded for the poor, in their rooms or flats. Divorce was quite usual and easy. Many people married more than once – either for love or for money.

We know a lot about Roman family life because in August, 79 AD the volcano Vesuvius erupted and completely buried the small town of Pompeii, near Rome. When it was uncovered, archaeologists could see the town almost as it was on that terrible day – the meals still on the tables, the goods in the shops and people lying where they fell! Some of the pictures in this book come from Pompeii.

Parents The pictures show a typical Ancient Roman man and woman — dark-eyed and handsome. The father was the head of the family. He could be very strict and he had great power. If his wife or children displeased him, he could make them slaves or even put them to death! The mother's job was to make sure that the household ran smoothly.

Children If a baby was weak or diseased, its father could order it to be exposed on a hillside until it died. Romans longed for boy babies but girls were regarded as rather useless. Children wore lucky charms to keep off evil spirits. Girls wore them until they married and boys until they came of age at fourteen. The hairpin with the hand decoration is a lucky charm.

Marriage Romans often married when they were still children. A girl could marry when she was twelve and a boy when he was fourteen. They were often betrothed even younger. A daughter of the Emperor Claudius was betrothed when she was only one! Marriages were usually arranged by the parents. Weddings were occasions for great celebration. The drawing shows a part of it – a bride being brought to her new home accompanied by friends, relatives and music. Like modern brides, she wore white, had a ring and was carried over the threshold. But her shoes and her veil were orange.

Clothes

Children generally wore tunics, like this sleepy little boy. For best they dressed up in *togas*. The simple but elegant toga was made out of one enormous sheet wound round the body. Cloaks were useful in the cold winter weather. But Romans wore hats only in the countryside during the summer, as protection from the strong sunshine. No-one wore shoes inside. Out of doors, men wore heavy boots with metal studs or sandals that laced up the leg. Women and children wore sandals like this very well-preserved one. Children didn't have underwear. But they put on warm woolly trousers in winter.

13

Jewellery Romans adored jewellery. Men, women and children decked themselves with necklaces, armbands, rings and earrings if they could afford them. Here is some of the jewellery they wore. Brooches like the bronze bird were worn to keep shawls and cloaks in place. Jewellery was made out of gold, silver, bronze and other metals.

Hairstyles Women and girls prided themselves on their beautiful hair. As you can see, Roman hairstyles were very ornate. They were kept in place by pins and combs like these. Imagine having to spend an hour or two having your hair done each morning!

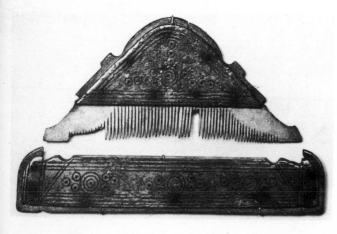

Health There were doctors in Ancient Roman days, though they were very different from ours! But, if these pictures are to be believed, they were just as concerned and kind. They did not know how to cure serious illnesses and injuries, so most Romans died young. Herbs were used for medicines and spa waters were popular too. The

Roman writer Pliny said they could "cure the insane ... are good for gallstones ... clear up acne ... induce memory". Of course there were no dentists with painless drills. A child's aching tooth was just pulled out as quickly as possible. Some Romans had false teeth made out of cement. They can't have been very comfortable!

C 281

Slaves   Unless the family was very poor, there were slaves for every job. Children had their own slaves who dressed them, played with them and took them to school. Slaves were usually foreigners. They were bought and sold in the marketplace and worked as servants for no wages. But often they were treated kindly as part of the family. Pliny must have been a good master. He says: "I know that most people think the death of a slave is like the loss of a valuable animal and nothing more. People who think that are hardly human."

Pets   Roman children loved pets as much as we do today. They were fond of keeping dogs, like the one in the picture, or cage birds. Parrots were brought to Rome by travellers for the rich. Poorer families put finches or thrushes in their cages. Sometimes Romans kept pet mice but never cats — they were thought unlucky.

2. Home Life

Roman homes were very different from our own. The houses were airy and cool with not much furniture because Rome is very hot most of the year. Rich families had fine decorations on their floors and walls and cool courtyard gardens. Poorer families had to manage in one bare room in a crowded block of flats. Life in the country was comfortable for those who could afford a nice villa and farm. But most country people lived in primitive shacks.

Winters could be quite cold in Rome. Then the Romans used their *hypocausts,* a very good type of central heating. Hot air from a furnace under the floors travelled up through hollow walls to heat the rooms. But the Romans didn't invent electricity and they had to use candles and oil lamps for lighting in the evenings. To save money, they usually got up at the crack of dawn and went to bed at sunset. Winter must have been a dull time!

When it came to food, the rich Romans had plenty of exotic things to eat. But once again the poor fared badly. They just had boring stodge. I think you can guess that the picture shows a very wealthy family at home!

Food The Ancient Romans ate three meals a
day. Their main meal was eaten at half past two. It
was called *cena* and it could go on for hours.
Sometimes there might be as many as seven
courses! Rich families enjoyed such delicacies as
peacocks, stuffed sows' udders, flamingoes boiled
with dates and dormice stuffed with pine nuts!
The poor ate bread or porridge for almost every
meal. Their food was very dull. The bread was
black and coarse, and there was no sugar to put
on the porridge. Country people ate better. They
grew plenty of fruit and vegetables.

24

Dinner Parties There were usually nine guests at a Roman dinner party. The most important one sat next to the host. Notice how the Romans ate their meal almost lying down. It doesn't look very comfortable! In between courses, poets, singers, musicians and dancers kept the guests amused. When it was a child's birthday, the house was filled with flowers and candles, and incense was burned in every room. Relatives were invited to a great feast and everyone gave presents. Even after people died, the family still celebrated their birthdays.

25

Drink Everyone, including the children, drank wine, though it was usually watered down or mixed with honey to make it sweeter. Pliny said that there were over two hundred different kinds of wine. It was made by farmers from grapes grown in the country and sold in the towns in shops like this.

26

Utensils   This picture of cooking utensils found in Pompeii shows you just how many pots and pans the Roman cook used. They were made out of metals such as copper. Roman pottery was much admired. It could be very plain. Sometimes it was ornate. This pretty little jug, used for holding oil, shows a woman washing her hair while her daughter plays with the soap bubbles.

Slimming If they could afford it, Romans were very greedy. There are even tales of people making themselves sick on purpose so that they could eat more! There must have been a lot of fat Romans, but sometimes you hear of dieters. A Greek doctor called Galen advised eating raw vegetables in vinegar to lose weight! You can see him talking to some plump Romans in the picture.

Lamps The Romans had no electricity so they used candles and little clay lamps like these. The lamps were very simple but effective. One had as many as fourteen wicks and, according to a Roman called Maltias, it could "light up an entire feast with its flames". Rich families kept their homes well-lit. They could afford the oil to fill their lamps. The poor went to bed early.

31

Mosaics The Romans decorated their floors and pavements with mosaics. Mosaics are pictures made out of tiny pieces of marble, stone or tiles. Some are patterned, like this pavement. Others tell stories about the gods the Romans believed in. Romans called the wall paintings in their houses frescoes. The bright pictures told stories either about the family or the gods. This one shows Venus, the goddess of love, talking to a young bride. She is no doubt giving her good advice on how to control her husband!

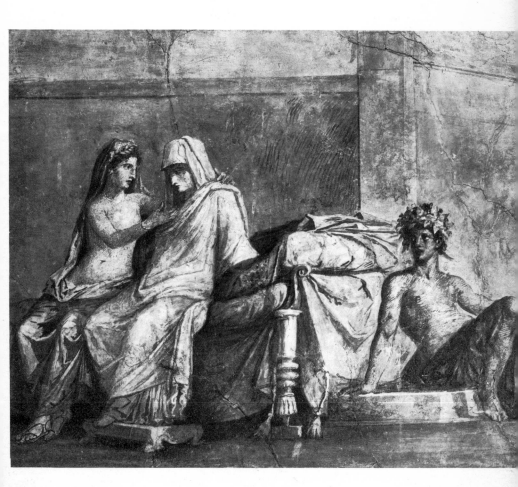

Statues Romans loved statues and busts (head-and-shoulders statues). It was a sign of wealth to have as many as possible. Rich families' houses were full of them. So were the streets and public buildings. The statues were usually of members of the family or famous people. This one is of the Emperor Hadrian. He lived a hundred years after Christ and had a famous long wall built while on a visit to Britain. Perhaps Roman children preferred to have the little figures as ornaments.

Gardens Most townspeople had gardens but they were rather different from our own. As you can see from this picture, they were full of statues, birds and exotic plants. The gentleman looks well-organized with his canopy to protect him from the sun. Poor families who lived in flats had to be content with "miniature gardens in boxes", as Pliny called them. Romans didn't think that children needed special play areas.

FECER

3. And so to School

Until the age of seven, boys and girls were looked after by their mothers and nurses. Not everybody thought this was a good idea. Pliny, who lived in the first century AD, wrote: "As soon as our children are born, we hand them over to some silly Greek maidservant." That was unfair. Greek nurses or tutors were popular because they were clever at reading and playing music.

Only the rich could afford to send their children to school. Most children had no education. First, schoolchildren went to an elementary school where they learned oratory, the art of public of course) and do sums. Then they went to a grammar school where they learned long poems off by heart, made speeches, and learned how to hunt, ride, shoot and fight. The only foreign language they learned was Greek. Very clever children went on to rhetoric school (like our college) where they learned oratory, the art of public speaking.

Of course it was usually only the boys who went to school. Most girls stayed at home. They were taught by their mothers how to be good wives and housekeepers. Girls also learned skills such as singing and sewing.

Schooling This carving shows the education of a small boy before he went to school. His parents taught him everything. When they were seven, children began their real schooling. Boys, and some girls, went first to elementary school (primary), then grammar school (secondary) and finished up in a rhetoric school (a sort of college) if they were very clever.

M·CORNELIO·M·F·PAL·STATIO·P   FFECER·

Telling the Time Most children left for school before it was light. A slave carried a lantern and their books. Breakfast, a steaming hot roll from a street stall, was eaten on the way. During the day they could tell the time by using sundials. Some people had water clocks which worked the same way as an egg timer. In the summer, school ended at midday. Here is a portable Roman lantern.

Teachers In Ancient Rome, teachers were very badly paid and not much respected. Often they were Greek slaves who had been given their freedom. They were much stricter than today. It was believed that "any man who has not been flogged has not been trained". Judging by this picture, Aristotle was right when he said "all learning is painful".

Lessons All schoolchildren learned the three Rs – reading, writing and arithmetic. They learned Latin, which was the language spoken in Rome, and Greek. If they went on to rhetoric school they learned such strange subjects as public speaking, philosophy and logic.

Writing Roman children didn't have exercise books and biros. They wrote with a stylus. One end of it was pointed for writing words. Children wrote on wax-coated wooden tablets, similar to the one in the picture. At the end of the lesson the children could warm their tablets and rub off the writing with the blunt end of the stylus.

Scrolls The two pupils in the picture are reading from scrolls. Romans didn't have printed books. They joined sheets of paper together and rolled them up like this. Their paper was made from papyrus (Egyptian reed) or vellum (animal skins rubbed with pumice and chalk). They wrote on the paper with a stylus dipped in ink.

Girls Some girls went to elementary school with their brothers. Many could read and write. As you can see, the young girl in the picture is reading a scroll. But most girls stayed at home and learned how to be good housewives. Their mothers taught them how to sing, dance, sew and cook.

Army Training Boys often learned their jobs from their fathers, and followed the same trade. But it was the dream of every young boy to join the famous Roman army. Their fathers taught them how to fight and defend themselves. Then when they were fourteen they could become soldiers. Army life was tough but exciting. Soldiers had to be exceptionally fit. They had to walk miles every day, live off porridge and travel all over the world conquering new lands.

4. Town and Country

Roman towns were far ahead of their time. Before the birth of Christ, they had sewage systems with drains along the streets and public toilets with stone seats! Roads were paved and cobbled. If the town was big and wealthy, like Rome itself, there were many useful and beautiful buildings — temples, libraries and government offices.

Town life was crowded and bustling. There was always something for children to do and see, like the victory parade in the picture. But the noise was tremendous. This is an account from a man who lived over the public baths: "The hair plucker ... he's never quiet unless he's working and then he's plucking armpits and his victim does his yelling for him ... outside a carpenter, up that street a blacksmith ... and last but not least, the maker of musical instruments ... always testing his oboes and trumpets ... Let's face it, only the rich sleep nowadays."

In the countryside the pace was much slower — and quieter! Most people were farmers. They grew enough food to feed their families and took the extra to the forum (market place) in the town. Everyone, including the children, had to work very hard. They may not have agreed with Cicero that "Of all the ways of making money, nothing is better than agriculture." Cicero was an orator, not a farmer.

Shops

The narrow streets of Rome were crammed with shops. By 300 AD there were over 2,300. A comic poet called Plautus wrote: "Wherever you go you see ... the jeweller, the wool seller, the man selling lingerie and bridal veils, violet or yellow dye ... shoes smelling of balsam ...

cobblers squatting on their heels, men selling slippers and sandals . . .'' In these pictures you can see the shoemaker, the ropemaker and the blacksmith working peacefully. But the woman in the butcher's shop looks a fussy customer and the toga shop seems to have a whole family to please.

Bakers Bread was baked and sold in the same shop. Though housewives ground their own flour, not many homes had ovens. The women brought their bread and other meals to be cooked at the bakery. Bakers were highly respected because bread was such an important part of the Roman diet. Baker's children often became bakers too.

Money In early times Romans didn't use coins. They paid for good with metal bars or exchanged them for other goods. About 200 BC a silver coin was introduced called the *denarius.* It was worth about 4p. Most coins had the emperor's head on them. Can you see Julius Caesar and Pompey the Great on two of these coins? Top left is a denarius.

51

Fullers People who washed clothes were called *fullers*. The dirty clothes were put in big tubs of water and trodden on until they were clean. Then they were bleached over a pan of horrible-smelling sulphur. Finally, they were pressed. In Rome, the fullers were men.

Streets   Most streets were noisy and crowded.
Few were paved. Flats overhung the streets, block-
ing out the light. But some streets, such as the
Appian Way in this drawing, were spacious and
elegant. Wealthy people were carried about on
litters (rather like sedan chairs) by up to six slaves.
Vehicles were not allowed in the streets during the
day, but at night the noise of carriage wheels was
deafening for children trying to go to sleep.

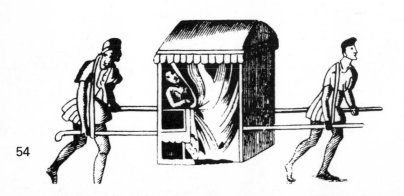

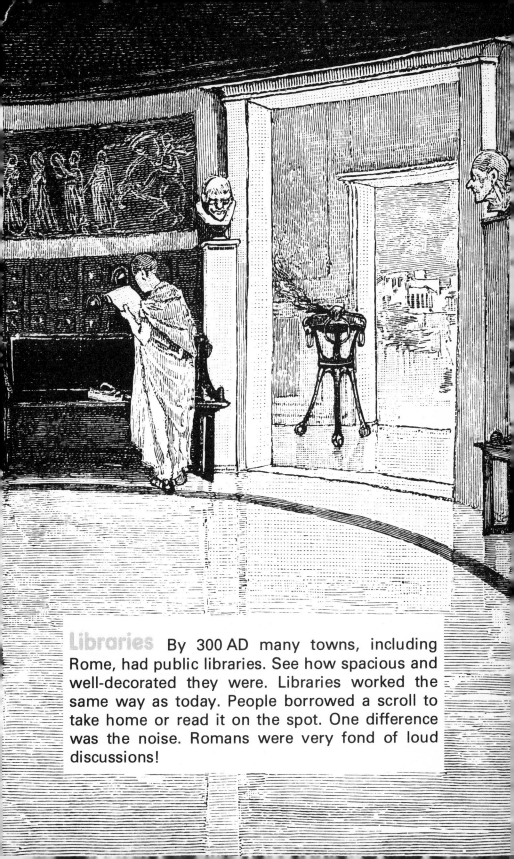

Libraries By 300 AD many towns, including Rome, had public libraries. See how spacious and well-decorated they were. Libraries worked the same way as today. People borrowed a scroll to take home or read it on the spot. One difference was the noise. Romans were very fond of loud discussions!

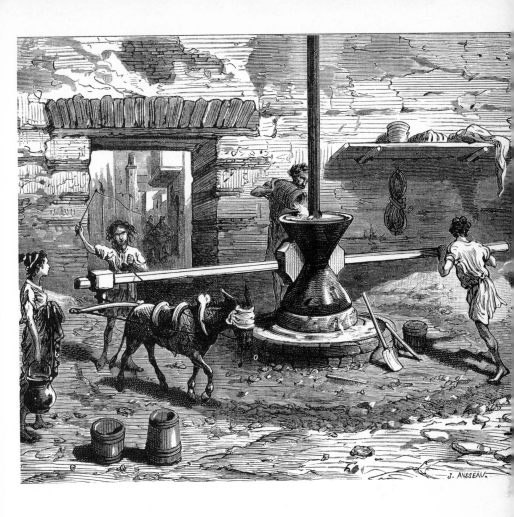

Farmers It was the farmers' job to feed the townspeople, so they were an important part of Roman life. They kept cows, sheep and chickens. Wheat was the most important crop. They also grew barley, rye and oats. Their method of grinding corn certainly looks different from ours. Children helped their parents as soon as they could walk. Usually they looked after the animals.

Vines Grapes were grown everywhere possible. You will remember that Romans were great wine drinkers. Children enjoyed treading the ripe grapes to squeeze out the juice. Olives were another important fruit. They were eaten raw or pressed to make oil. The Romans cooked their food in olive oil. Roman children had to eat up their cabbage and spinach, too. But they didn't know about potatoes, tomatoes or bananas.

Aqueducts The "bridge" in this picture is really an *aqueduct,* a structure for carrying water not for going over it! It was built by the Romans to bring water from country springs into a town. Lead pipes were connected to the aqueducts so that the rich families could have running water and flushing toilets. The poor had to carry water from the street well. There wasn't much to spare for poor children to wash at home.

5. Toys, Sports and Amusements

The Ancient Romans adored being entertained. It didn't matter whether it was a simple game of dice at home or a visit to the theatre – they really enjoyed themselves.

Children played many games we still play today. Leap-frog and blind man's buff were especially popular. They played dice too, though they would be soundly whipped if they were found gambling! Sometimes the children would be allowed to take part in the dinner parties enjoyed by their parents. They could also go to the baths, like the families in the picture.

There were entertainments to which all the family would go, such as *gladiator* fights at the Colosseum. They were often cruel and bloodthirsty shows, as Seneca wrote: "'Kill', they shouted, 'Beat him! Why won't he face the sword? What a coward! Why can't he die eagerly? Beat his wounded back! They must strike each other's bare chests! Oh, it's the interval, well let's have someone strangled. We must have something to watch!'"

Special shows were put on when it was a public holiday for a god's feast day or the emperor's birthday. People didn't have to pay to see them – they just had to make sure that they got there early to fight for a seat!

The Baths Roman families went to the baths to gossip, meet their friends, eat and drink — and get clean of course! There were three sorts of baths. The frigidarium was very cold. The tepidarium was warm. And the caldarium was very hot. People went into each bath in turn and perhaps had a massage afterwards. It was very refreshing. During the emperor Diocletian's reign a bath was built which could hold three thousand people. The bath in the picture was built by the Romans in Britain during the first century AD at a place now called — Bath!

Amphitheatres

A big stadium where gladiator and animal fights took place was called an *amphitheatre*. You can see from the top picture that amphitheatres were built in the round with raised seats and a tunnel through which the fighters came. The biggest amphitheatre in Rome was the Colosseum, which could hold 55,000 spectators. When it first opened in the first century AD, there were a hundred days of non-stop entertainment. The picture below shows you its size.

Gladiators Slaves or prisoners were carefully trained to fight men or animals. They were called gladiators. You can see the helmet and special belt the gladiators wore for protection if you look at the vase. Gladiators had to be very brave as fights were to the death. If the emperor decided that the gladiator had fought well and was just about to be killed, he could give the "thumbs up" sign, which meant that his life was saved. If he gave the "thumbs down" sign, the gladiator was killed.

Animal Fights Another popular entertainment was animal fighting. Men fought wild animals, animals fought animals, and prisoners were thrown to starving beasts. The carving shows gladiators fighting lions, and in the mosaic they are fighting leopards. You can see how the animals were prodded to make them even more angry. The people in the little boxes were probably the emperor and his family. Not everyone enjoyed these blood-baths. Most children preferred exhibitions of such exotic creatures as ostriches, hippopotamuses and rhinoceroses, or watching performing animals. We even hear of tightrope-walking elephants.

Chariot Races Children loved the danger-
ous chariot races which took place in amphitheatres. There were four teams — the whites, the
blues, the greens and the reds. Each chariot was
drawn by four horses. The charioteer wore a crash

helmet. He tied the reins around his body but he had a little knife to free himself in case he got caught up. The Romans placed bets on the team they thought would win as a trumpeter signalled the start of each race.

Theatres Children enjoyed watching the "pantomimes" – actors miming. But their plays were more like musicals than the Christmas shows we call pantomimes today. The theatre in the photograph was built by the Romans in Spain, which was part of their empire. Theatres put on other shows, too. People went to them to watch boxing matches or striptease acts. The boxers wore gloves spiked with metal to give an extranasty punch, and special straps on their wrists.

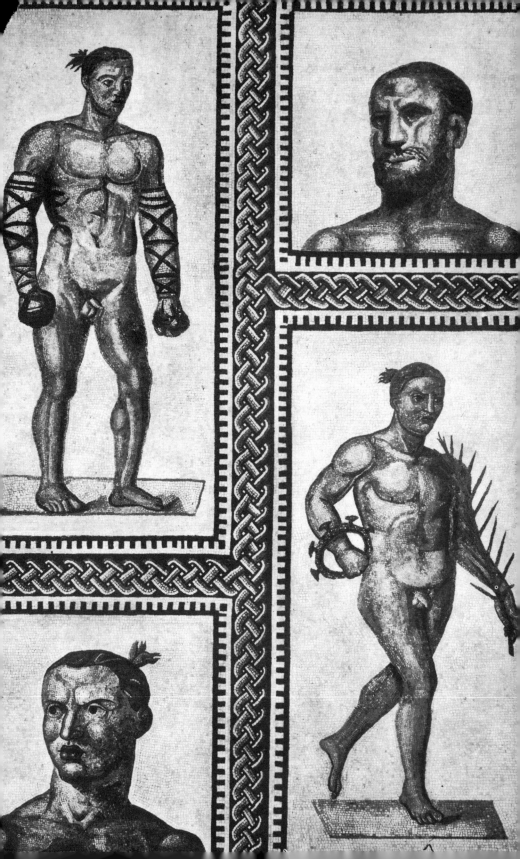

72

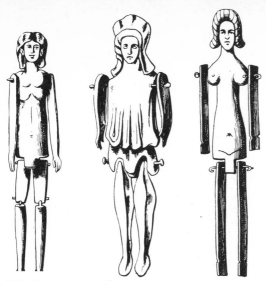

Children's Games

Children played many games that are still popular today. They used nuts to roll like marbles. The statue of the little girl playing knucklebones should tell you how the game got its name. We call it jacks or fivestones today. Roman children had jointed dolls, rather like our puppets. The little toys were found in a Roman child's grave. Some of them may have been used to hold oil too. Can you see the spouts on the animal figures?

Travel The Romans believed that travel to other countries broadened their ideas. The Seven Wonders of the World were great attractions for the wealthy Roman family. They were the Pyramids, the Statue of Jupiter at Athens, the Colossus at Rhodes, the Mausoleum at Halicarnassus, the Hanging Gardens of Babylon, the Temple of Diana at Ephesus and the Pharos of Alexandria. We can still see the Pyramids but the other wonders have not survived.

40

6. The Old Gods

The Ancient Romans were pagans. This means. they believed in more than one god. In fact, they believed in hundreds! There were gods and goddesses for everything from love to war. Each family worshipped a special household god. They kept little statues of household gods on altars in the house. It was important to keep all the gods happy, so the Romans gave them presents and made sacrifices to them. They also celebrated with festivals for the gods. Often the festivals became public holidays.

The Romans believed in an after-life. When they died, coins were placed in their mouths for paying the ferryman to row them over the River Styx to the Underworld, where all the dead souls lived. Sometimes the Romans were buried with some of their possessions so that they could continue to use them in the next life. Remember the toys found in the child's grave.

In 324 AD the emperor Constantine declared that the official Roman religion was to be Christianity. He moved his capital to what is now Istanbul (he called it Constantinople) and Rome itself was invaded by the barbarians in the fifth century. But Rome later became the centre of the Christian religion and the seat of the popes.

The statue opposite is Mars, the Roman god of war.

GIOVE SERAPIDE

The Gods The Romans worshipped all sorts of gods. The chief ones were Jupiter, Mars, Apollo, Neptune and Mercury. There were also goddesses. Juno, Minerva, Diana and Venus were four of the most important. Their home was Mount Olympus in Greece. The vase shows you Neptune, the god of the sea, and Mercury, the god of trade and the messenger of the other gods. The bust is of Jupiter, father of the gods. Below, you can see children making a sacrifice to Diana, the moon goddess. Her statue is on the column.

Mithras The god worshipped by the army was Mithras. He was a Persian god and legend has it that he was born out of a rock. Only the bravest men could become his followers. First they had to go through many painful ordeals, such as spending the night in a cramped box, which was placed in water to make things worse. Statues of Mithras killing a bull have been found in temples throughout the Roman empire.

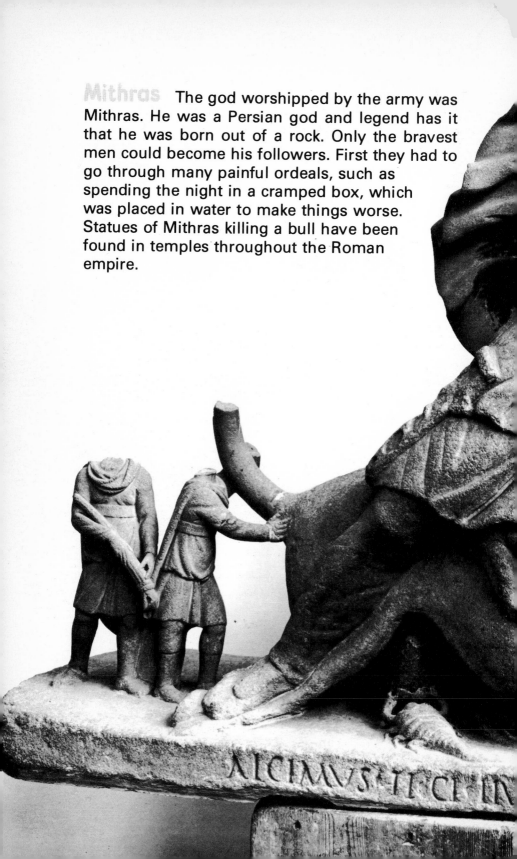

Emperor Gods Augustus was such a good emperor that many Romans thought he must have been a god. Other emperors, too were deified (worshipped as gods) after they died, and temples were built for them. One of the most impressive was the temple built for the emperor Claudius in

Colchester. Not much remains today, but this reconstruction shows you what it was like. Vespasian, the emperor who built the Colosseum, said on his death-bed, "Good Heavens! I really think I'm turning into a god." And some emperors, like Julius Caesar, said their ancestors were gods.

Vestal Virgins Temples dedicated to Vesta, the goddess of the hearth, were looked after by six Vestal Virgins. It was their job to make sure that the sacred flame never went out. Very young girls were chosen. "It is not legal if she is less than 6 years or more than 10 . . . She must not have any impediment in speech or hearing . . . or have anything else wrong with her body . . . Neither of her parents must have been slaves." This painting shows a school for Vestal Virgins. Sometimes children were special attendants at sacrifices in other temples. A boy attendant (right) was called a *camillus* and a girl a *camilla*.

Festivals Every god and goddess had his or her own special day. The festival of Flora is being celebrated in this picture. It was a spring festival and Romans decorated their houses with flowers and wore garlands for a week. There were other special days, too. There was a sort of Mother's Day on 1st March, and in May ghosts of dead relatives were said to return to haunt their families on three days.

Saturnalia The most important festival was *Saturnalia*, held in honour of Saturn, who was the father of Jupiter, and the god of agriculture and civilization. It lasted from 17th to 22nd December and during that time everyone was on holiday. Schools were closed, presents were exchanged and of course there was a lot of eating and drinking. Masters served their slaves, who were not allowed to do any work for once. In some ways, it was rather like our Christmas. But the picture shows a wilder scene than most Christmas parties.

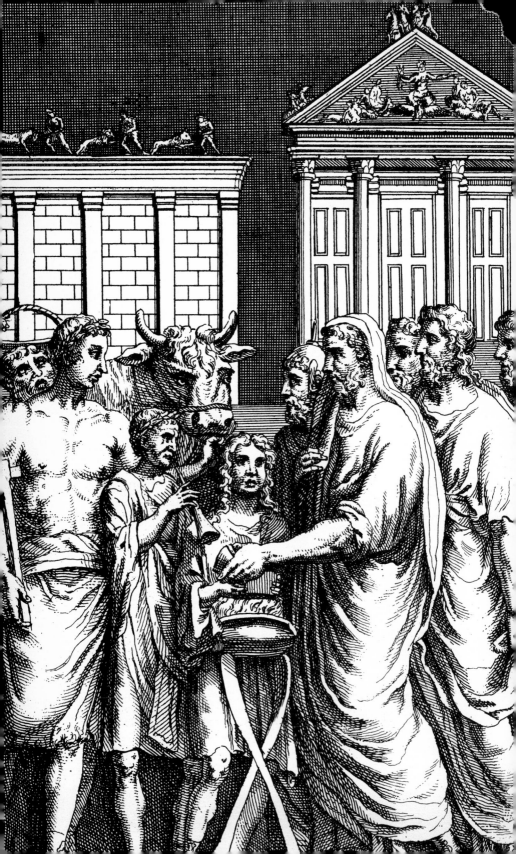

Soothsayers People who claimed to see into the future and tell fortunes were called soothsayers. They read horoscopes and gave advice. The Romans were very superstitious and thought that soothsayers had magical powers. Sometimes people watched chickens eating to tell the future. If the chickens attacked their food hungrily, it was a good omen. But if they only picked at it, that was a bad sign. These Romans are studying omens.

Funerals When Romans died, they were given very elaborate funerals. The body was carried through the streets on a litter, dressed in its best toga. If it was a child's funeral, flute players led the procession. If it was an adult's, there were trumpeters. Many people were cremated. The remains were placed in an incinerary urn like this. Rich people had magnificent roadside tombs but the poor were just shovelled into a public pit.

New Words

Amphitheatre	A stadium where Romans watched gladiator fights.
Aqueduct	A structure for carrying water into towns
Camillus	A boy attendant at a sacrifice; a girl was called *camilla*
Cena	The main meal in Rome, eaten about half past two in the afternoon
Denarius	A Roman coin worth about 4p
Frescoes	Wall paintings
Fullers	Launderers
Gladiators	Men trained to fight with weapons
Hypocaust	A central heating system
Mosaics	Pictures made out of tiny pieces of stone, marble or tiles
Saturnalia	The festival for the god Saturn, held in December
Toga	A gown made out of a single piece of material

More Books

Ancient Rome by N Sherwin White (Longman, 1959). A very useful book with lots of information.

A Roman Town by R J Unstead (Hutchinson, 1977). An excellent book, suitable for all ages.

Everyday Life in Roman and Anglo-Saxon Times by M & C H B Quennell (Batsford, 1959). Packed full of detail and interesting stories.

Gladiators by M Grant (Penguin, 1971). An interesting book for the older reader seeking more detail. A good picture section.

Life in Roman Britain by A Birley (Batsford, 1964). A good book, specializing in one part of the Roman empire. Lots of excellent photographs.

The Roman People by E K Milliken (Harrap, 1952). A very detailed book, suitable for older readers.

The Romans by Joan Forman (Macdonald Educational, 1975). Lively, well-drawn pictures. Full of information.

The Story of Rome by L C Corney (E Arnold, 1964). A clearly-presented history of Rome. Good for younger readers.

Index

Picture Credits